The Only Cookbook You Need

Recipes to Start Cooking Chicken the Right Way

BY

MOLLY MILLS

Copyright © 2019 by Molly Mills

License Notes

No part of this book may be copied, replicated, distributed, sold or shared without the express and written consent of the Author.

The ideas expressed in the book are for entertainment purposes. The Reader assumes all risk when following any guidelines and the Author accepts no responsibility if damages occur due to actions taken by the Reader.

An Amazing Offer for Buying My Book!

Thank you very much for purchasing my books! As a token of my appreciation, I would like to extend an amazing offer to you! When you have subscribed with your e-mail address, you will have the opportunity to get free and discounted e-books that will show up in your inbox daily. You will also receive reminders before an offer expires so you never miss out. With just little effort on your part, you will have access to the newest and most informative books at your fingertips. This is all part of the VIP treatment when you subscribe below.

SIGN ME UP: *https://molly.gr8.com*

Table of Contents

Chicken Recipes 7

Recipe 1: Grilled Chicken with Whiskey-Ginger Marinade 8

Recipe 2: Spicy Chicken Quesadillas 11

Recipe 3: Tequila Lime Chicken Enchiladas 13

Recipe 4: General Tso's Chicken 16

Recipe 5: Chicken Stuffing Casserole 19

Recipe 6: Honey Sesame Chicken 21

Recipe 7: Chicken Santa Fe 24

Recipe 8: Chicken Lo Mein 26

Recipe 9: Crockpot Chicken and Herb Dumplings 29

Recipe 10: Chicken filled Lettuce Wrap 32

Recipe 11: Caribbean Dump Chicken 36

Recipe 12: Enchilada Chicken Mango Salad 38

Recipe 13: Honey- Whiskey Chicken Wings 40

Recipe 14: Asian-Inspired Chicken Wings 43

Recipe 15: Whiskey Orange Chipotle Chicken 46

Recipe 16: Sautéed Chicken Breasts with Chive Sauce 49

Recipe 17: Chicken Tequila Burgers 51

Recipe 18: Chinese Chicken Noodle 54

Recipe 19: Apricot Tequila Glazed Drumsticks 57

Recipe 20: Moo Shu Chicken Wraps 59

Recipe 21: Chicken Tequila Fettuccine 62

Recipe 22: Chicken Taco Salad 65

Recipe 23: Plantain Chip Nachos 68

Recipe 24: Chicken and Avocado Tostadas 70

Recipe 25: Chicken and Cornmeal Dumplings 73

Recipe 26: Mexican Chicken Soup with Cheddar Cheese Chips 76

About the Author 79

Don't Miss Out! 81

Chicken Recipes

AAAAAAAAAAAAAAAAAAAAAAAAAAAAAAAAAAAAAAAA

Recipe 1: Grilled Chicken with Whiskey-Ginger Marinade

Delicious main course, easy to make and will be enjoyed by the whole family, may be served with rice or roasted potatoes.

Yield: 4

Cooking Time: 60 minutes

List of Ingredients:

- Soy Sauce (1/3 cup)
- Hoisin sauce (2 Tbsp.)
- Lime Juice (2 Tbsp.)
- Ginger (2 tsp., grated)
- Red Pepper (¼ tsp., minced)
- Olive Oil cooking spray
- Cornstarch (½ tsp.)
- Brown Sugar (3 Tbsp.)
- Sesame Oil (2 tsp.)
- Garlic (2 cloves, crushed)
- Water (1 Tbsp.)
- Sesame Seeds (1 tsp., toasted)
- Boneless Chicken Breasts (1 ounce, boneless)
- Whiskey (1/3 cup)

AAAAAAAAAAAAAAAAAAAAAAAAAAAAAAAAAAAAAAAA

Instructions:

1. Wrap each chicken breast with plastic wrap and pound until the meat is ½ inch thick

2. Mix Whiskey, Soy sauce, Hoisin sauce, Lime Juice, Ginger, Red Pepper, Brown Sugar, Sesame Oil and Garlic. Place the chicken breast in a Ziploc bag and pour the marinade on the stripes. Leave refrigerated for one hour.

3. Warm up the grill and remove the marinade meat from the refrigerator.

4. Spray the cooking spray on the grill, each chicken stripe should be grilled for five minutes.

5. Once all stripes are completed, place on a platter and slice thinly

6. Boil water, cornstarch and the marinade mix, leave to simmer for 10 minutes.

7. Pour the mixture over the chicken stripes and sprinkle sesame seeds

8. Serve & Enjoy!

Recipe 2: Spicy Chicken Quesadillas

Cheesy quesadillas are great for anytime and you can get as creative as you like. Add as many Mexican toppings and spices as you like and enjoy.

Yield: 4-6

Cooking Time: 20 minutes

List of Ingredients:

- Paleo Tortillas (12)
- Coconut oil (2 Tbsp.)
- Jalapeño (4, chopped)
- Cheddar cheese (6 slices)
- Sundried tomatoes (2 Tbsp.)
- Cilantro (1 Tbsp.)
- Organic sour cream

AAAAAAAAAAAAAAAAAAAAAAAAAAAAAAAAAAAAAA

Instructions:

Lay one tortilla flat and fill with tomato, jalapeno, cheese and top with oil. Repeat for as many as you need, you could also add cooked meat if you so desire.

Bake for 15 minutes and remove from flame. Top with sour cream and enjoy!

Recipe 3: Tequila Lime Chicken Enchiladas

Enjoy this warm Mexican dish with a slight citrus tequila bland. This chicken enchilada will be a great addition for the next dinner party with friends.

Yield: 4-6

Cooking Time: 30 minutes

List of Ingredients:

- Chicken breast (3, deboned and skinless)
- Lime juice (¼ cup)
- Salsa (½ cup)
- Olive oil (2 Tbsp.)
- Tortillas (1 bag)
- Tequila (¼ cup)
- Lime Rind (1 tsp., grated)
- Salt (¼ tsp.)
- Mexican cheese (1 cup, shredded)
- Black pepper (¼ tsp.)
- Enchilada sauce (1 cup)

Instructions:

1. Cube chicken and put into a bowl along with lime juice and tequila. Place in fridge for half hour.

2. Heat oil in a skillet and sauté chicken until browned then ad all leftover ingredients except cheese and tortillas.

3. Lay tortilla flat and top with cook chicken and cheese. Roll and place into baking dish along with enchilada sauce. Top with extra cheese and bake for 10-15 minutes or until cheese melts.

4. Remove from heat, serve and enjoy!

Recipe 4: General Tso's Chicken

The Chinese food menu is never complete without the famous General's Tso's Chicken. This scrumptious chicken derived from China many years ago; it is said it was named in orientation to a brave General.

Yield: 2

Cooking Time: 30 minutes

List of Ingredients:

- Chicken Breast (10 oz., cubed)
- Shaoxing wine (½ Tbsp.)
- Salt (¼ tsp.)
- Cornstarch (1/3 cup)
- Oil (1 tbsp.)
- Ginger (3 slices, minced)
- Garlic (1 clove, diced)
- Red Chilies (5, seeds removed)
- Scallion (2 stalks, white parts)

Sauce

- Chinese rice vinegar (3 Tbsp.)
- Soy Sauce (2 ½ Tbsp.)
- Dark soy sauce (½ Tbsp.)
- Hoisin Sauce (1 tsp.)
- Sugar (2 ½ Tbsp.)
- Water (¼ cup)
- Shaoxing Wine (½ Tbsp.)
- Cornstarch (1 Tbsp.)

AAAAAAAAAAAAAAAAAAAAAAAAAAAAAAAAAAAAAAAAA

Instructions:

Cover meat in a container with salt and wine; let it marinate for 15 minutes. Mix together ingredients for the sauce and put aside till needed. Heat oil and put cornstarch on chicken. Cook chicken until browned. Remove from pot with a slotted spoon and place on paper towels to absorb excess oil.

Using another pan or wok, heat 1 ½ Tbsp. of oil, then add ginger, chilies and garlic. Cook until chilies are fragrant. Put sauce into wok/pan and cook till sauce gets thick then add chicken. Stir to combine and add scallion.

Serve hot.

Recipe 5: Chicken Stuffing Casserole

Yield: 3 – 4

Cooking Time: 6 – 7 hours

List of Ingredients:

- Chicken breasts (4-6, deboned and skinned)
- Broccoli (10 oz., chopped)
- Chicken broth (½ cup)
- Chicken stuffing (1 box)
- Cheesy broccoli soup (1 can)
- Butter

Instructions:

1. Set slow cooker on low.

2. Use butter to grease slow cooker and then add chicken.

3. Combine all remaining ingredients and pour all over chicken.

4. Cover pot and cook for 6-7 hours.

Recipe 6: Honey Sesame Chicken

This dish is effortless and very satisfying. The honey chicken is filled with savory, sticky and syrupy honey goodness.

Yield: 2

Cooking Time: 25 minutes

List of Ingredients:

- Chicken breasts (1 lb., cubed)
- Oil (1 tbsp.)
- Garlic (2 cloves, minced)
- Sesame seeds (toasted)

Batter (for frying)

- Egg white (1)
- Flour (½ cup, sifted)
- Cornstarch (¼ cup)
- Baking Powder (½ tsp.)
- Water (½ cup, cold)
- Oil (1 Tbsp.)
- Salt (pinch)

Honey Sesame Sauce

- Honey (1/3 cup)
- Apple Cider Vinegar (1 tsp.)
- Ketchup (½ Tbsp.)
- Sesame Oil (1 tsp.)
- Cornstarch (2 tsp.)
- Water (½ cup)
- Salt (1 tsp.)

AAAAAAAAAAAAAAAAAAAAAAAAAAAAAAAAAAAAAAAAA

Instructions:

Place ingredients for batter into a bowl and whip until batter is silky. Plunge chicken in and set aside. Mix ingredients for sauce in a separate container and put aside till needed.

Heat pan and add oil, then drop chicken in batter one piece at a time and fry till golden. Remove from pan with a slotted spoon and rest on hand towel.

Put 2 Tbsp. oil in a skillet and stir fry garlic till fragrant then add honey sauce and boil till it gets thick. Put in chicken and stir then add sesame seeds. Serve hot with white or fried rice.

Recipe 7: Chicken Santa Fe

Yield: 2 – 3

Cooking Time: 2 – 3 hours

List of Ingredients:

- Canned corn (15 oz., whole kernel)
- Chicken breasts (6, halved, deboned and skin removed)
- Canned black beans (15 oz., drained and rinsed)
- Cheddar cheese (1 cup, shredded)
- Salsa (1 cup, chunky)

Instructions:

1. Set slow cooker on high.

2. Combine corn, half of salsa and beans in slow cooker. Put in chicken and top with remaining salsa.

3. Cover pot and cook for 2 ½ -3 hours or until chicken is thoroughly cooked.

4. Top with cheese and cook for 5 minutes more or until cheese melts.

Recipe 8: Chicken Lo Mein

Lo Mein is a well-liked meal in Hong Kong that is served by combining boiled noodles with veggies, meat or wonton soup. This homemade Lo Mein is way beyond the class of the takeout edition you may be used to.

Yield: 2

Cooking Time: 20 minutes

List of Ingredients:

- Chinese noodles/ Spaghetti (8 oz.)
- Water
- Chicken Breast (8 oz., sliced)
- Cornstarch (1 tsp.)
- Oil (4 Tbsp.)
- Garlic (3 cloves, minced)
- Napa Cabbage (1 cup, sliced)
- Shiitake Mushroom (2, sliced)
- Carrots (1/3 cup, chopped)
- Chicken broth (½ cup)

Sauce

- So sauce (1 Tbsp.)
- Oyster Sauce (1 tsp.)
- Sesame Oil (¼ tsp.)
- White Pepper
- Sugar (½ tsp.)
- Salt (¼ tsp.)

AAAAAAAAAAAAAAAAAAAAAAAAAAAAAAAAAAAAAAAAA

Instructions:

Boil noodles as directed on package, drain and put aside till needed. Mix cornstarch with chicken and set aside.

Heat oil in a wok and brown garlic then add chicken, mushroom, cabbage, carrot and cook for 2 minutes. Put in broth and lower heat; reduce liquid and take away from flame. Add noodles, toss and serve hot.

Recipe 9: Crockpot Chicken and Herb Dumplings

Yield: 2 – 3

Cooking Time: 5 – 6 hours

List of Ingredients:

- Chicken (3 lbs.)
- Garlic (2 cloves, diced)
- Thyme powder (¼ tsp.)
- Dry white wine (½ cup)
- Biscuit mix (1 cup)
- Milk (6 Tbsp.)
- Salt (¼ tsp.)
- Marjoram powder (¼ tsp.)
- Black pepper (¼ tsp.)
- Bay leaf (1)
- Sour cream (1 cup)
- Parsley (1 Tbsp., chopped)
- Onions (10 small)

Instructions:

1. Set slow cooker on low.

2. Season chicken with pepper and salt. Put chicken into slow cooker.

3. Put garlic into pot along with onions, thyme, wine, marjoram and bay leaf.

4. Cover pot and cook for 5-6 hours.

5. Combine parsley and biscuit mix and add milk. Stir until mixture is moist. Drop spoons of mix into crock pot around the edge.

6. Set slow cooker on high and cook for 30 minutes.

Recipe 10: Chicken filled Lettuce Wrap

Lettuce wraps are simple chicken or pork mince wrapped in iceberg lettuce and served with a hoisin sauce for dipping. They are quick to prepare and great for your palate.

Yield: 4

Preparation: 20 minutes

List of Ingredients:

- Chicken breast (1 lb., ground)
- Mushrooms- shiitake (3, chopped)
- Garlic (3 cloves, diced)
- Water Chestnuts (2, minced)
- Oil (2 Tbsp.)

Marinade

- Soy Sauce (1 Tbsp.)
- Oyster Sauce (1 Tbsp.)
- Sweet soy sauce (½ tsp.)
- Salt (¼ tsp.)
- Shaoxing wine (1 Tbsp.)
- Corn Starch (1 tsp.)
- Scallion (1 stalk, diced)
- White Pepper (¼ tsp.)
- Iceberg Lettuce (1, cold)

Hoisin Dipping Sauce

- Hoisin Sauce (3 Tbsp.)
- Japanese ponzu sauce (1 Tbsp.)
- Sriracha chili sauce (½ tsp.)
- Water (1 Tbsp.)

Sweet Chili Sauce

- Sweet chili Sauce (4 Tbsp.)
- Cilantro leaves (chopped)
- Lime Juice (1/ Tbsp.)

AAAAAAAAAAAAAAAAAAAAAAAAAAAAAAAAAAAAAAAA

Instructions:

Combine mushrooms, chestnuts and meat together with marinade ingredients. Put aside for 15 minutes. Mix the chili and hoisin sauce and set aside.

Put oil in a pan or wok and heat then sauté garlic till golden. Once garlic is golden then add chicken and cook and remove from flame and set aside.

Take lettuce leaves off and spoon chicken into lettuce center. Serve by wrapping lettuce and dipping in chili or hoisin sauce or pouring sauce on before eating.

Recipe 11: Caribbean Dump Chicken

Delicious chicken without the hassle with the wonderful aromas and flavors of the Caribbean islands.

Yield: 3 – 4

Cooking Time: 4 - 6 hours

List of Ingredients:

- Brown sugar (¼ cup)
- Orange juice (1/3 cup)
- Chicken parts (1 ½ lbs.)
- Pineapple chunks in juice (8 oz.)
- Nutmeg (½ tsp.)
- Golden raisins (½ cup)

Instructions:

1. Put all ingredients into a large Ziploc bag and combine.

2. Freeze overnight and remove the next day. Thaw completely.

3. Set slow cooker to high/ low

4. Add contents to bag and cook for 6-8 hours on low or 4-6 hours on high until thoroughly cooked.

5. Chicken may also be baked at 350°F for 30-60 minutes.

Recipe 12: Enchilada Chicken Mango Salad

This is a quick and easy salad that you can make with any chicken of your choice. It is very fulfilling and the fruity mango blend great with the avocado.

Yield: 2

Cooking Time: 5 minutes

Carb: 4 g

List of Ingredients:

- Hearts of romaine (1 head, shredded)
- Enchilada chicken (1-2 cups)
- Mango (1, peeled and diced)
- Avocado (1, diced)
- Tomatoes
- Almonds/Walnuts
- Salt (¼ tsp.)
- Pepper (¼ tsp.)

AAAAAAAAAAAAAAAAAAAAAAAAAAAAAAAAAAAAAAA

Instructions:

Chop the romaine and put the chicken on top. Then add the avocado and mango on top along with tomatoes and top with almonds. Enjoy!

* You may also add more ingredients to the dish as you please (cranberries, cucumbers etc.)

Recipe 13: Honey- Whiskey Chicken Wings

If you are having small dinner party or a movie night, these honey-whiskey chicken wings are sure to start things of right. Grab a couple beers and Enjoy!

Yield: 12

Cooking Time: 60 minutes

List of Ingredients:

- Honey (3/4 cup)
- Dijon Mustard (¼ cup)
- Lime Zest (2 Tbsp., grated)
- Whiskey (¼ cup)
- Sugar (2 Tbsp.)
- Ancho Chili Powder (2 Tbsp.)
- Chicken Wings (2 dozen)
- Salt (½ tsp.)
- Pepper (¼ tsp.)

AAAAAAAAAAAAAAAAAAAAAAAAAAAAAAAAAAAAAAAA

Instructions:

1. Set oven to 450F

2. Place the wings on a baking sheet and season with salt and pepper

3. Roast in oven for 40 minutes until golden brown

4. In a saucepan on medium heat add honey, mustard and whiskey and bring to a simmer.

5. Mix sugar with lime zest, chili powder and 1 ½ tsp. of salt

6. Put the wings in a bowl and pour the whiskey sauce on top

7. Once coated, drizzle with the sugar mixture

8. Serve & Enjoy!

Recipe 14: Asian-Inspired Chicken Wings

Asian inspired wings that aren't sweet and sour or teriyaki but the fresh ingredients give it an Asian taste and feel that's to die for. If you can put these on the grill and barbecue them instead of baking they are even better.

Yield: 8

Cooking Time: 60 minutes

List of Ingredients:

- Chicken Wings (3 lbs.)
- Extra Virgin Coconut Oil (2 tbsp.)
- Garlic (4 cloves, chopped)
- Ginger (tbsp., chopped)
- Anise Seed (1 tsp)
- Fennel Seed (1 tsp)
- Coconut Aminos (½ cup)
- Honey (2 tbsp.)
- Apple Cider Vinegar (2 tbsp.)
- Fish Sauce (1 tbsp.)
- Sesame Oil (2 tbsp.)

AAAAAAAAAAAAAAAAAAAAAAAAAAAAAAAAAAAAAA

Instructions:

Put wings into a large bowl, drain or pat to dry. In a small saucepan heat oil then add garlic, ginger, fennel seed and anise and cook for 3 minutes.

Add honey, vinegar, aminos and fish sauce and cook for a minute. Remove from flame and add sesame oil. Pour mixture over wings and stir. Cool and refrigerate overnight, you may stir occasionally as it marinates.

Remove wings from marinade and bake wings at 375 °until they are done. Remove from heat and enjoy. Add your favorite side dish or have as is.

Recipe 15: Whiskey Orange Chipotle Chicken

When it comes to flavors this chicken will provide all that and more, it is very easy to make and it gives the chicken hours or days to soak all the flavors. At the first bit you will feel as if heaven has bene here on earth all along.

Yield: 6

Cooking Time: 75 minutes

List of Ingredients:

- Orange Marmalade (1 ½ cups)
- Whiskey (1 cup)
- Cilantro (½ bunch)
- Salt (1 Tbsp.)
- Black Pepper (1 Tbsp.)
- Chipotle Peppers in adobo sauce (8oz, 1 can)
- Tomato Paste (6oz, 1 can)
- Garlic (4 cloves, sliced)
- Olive Oil (1/3 cup)
- 6 chicken thighs
- 6 chicken legs

AAAAAAAAAAAAAAAAAAAAAAAAAAAAAAAAAAAAAAAAAA

Instructions:

1. Blend Olive Oil, Cilantro, Salt, Black Pepper, Garlic, Tomato Paste, Whiskey, Orange Marmalade, Chipotle Peppers and Adobo Sauce

2. Pour this mixture on the thighs and legs and let it marinade for 9hrs to 2 days.

3. Set oven to 400F

4. Lay the meat on baking tray cover with the chicken marinade and bake for 1 hour

5. Plate, serve and enjoy!

Recipe 16: Sautéed Chicken Breasts with Chive Sauce

This delicious chicken takes less than 30 minutes to get ready and can be served with a side of sautéed vegetables. The herbed sauce complements the simplicity of the chicken.

Yield: 4

Cooking Time: 20 minutes

List of Ingredients:

- Chicken breasts (4, cut in halves)
- Black pepper (¼ tsp.)
- Olive oil (1 Tbsp.)
- White wine (½ cup, dry)
- Chives (1 Tbsp., snipped)
- Salt (¼ tsp.)
- Whole wheat flour (3 Tbsp.)
- Shallots (½ cup, diced)
- Chicken stock (1 cup)

Instructions:

1. Use pepper and salt to season chicken breasts. Put flour into a dish and use to coat chicken thoroughly.

2. Heat oil in a skillet and cook for 5 minutes on one side until golden.

3. Flip chicken and cook for 5 minutes on the other side; remove from heat and put aside.

4. Prepare sauce by heating a skillet and cooking shallots for 2 minutes then add wine and cook for 1 minute until wine reduces by half. Use spoon to scrape pan.

5. Add broth to skillet and cook for 4 minutes, stir and cook until liquid reduces by half. Add chives and then add chicken. Heat thoroughly and serve.

Recipe 17: Chicken Tequila Burgers

These burgers are spicy and juicy and can be made for a barbecue or cookout as a treat for the adults. Put burgers on your favorite toasted bun and add toppings.

Yield: 2

Cooking Time: 20 minutes

List of Ingredients:

- Chicken breasts (2, cut into cubes)
- Cilantro (¼ cup, chopped)
- Lime zest
- Tequila (1 oz.)
- Oatmeal (¼ cup, plain)
- Garlic (1 clove, diced)
- Jalapeno pepper (3 tsp., diced)
- Soy sauce
- Salt (¼ tsp.)
- Black pepper (¼ tsp.)

AAAAAAAAAAAAAAAAAAAAAAAAAAAAAAAAAAAAAAAA

Instructions:

1. Set broiler and use foil to line a baking sheet. Use cooking spray to coat foil.

2. Put ingredients into food processor and pulse until combined and chicken ground.

3. Shape mixture into 2 balls and use hands to flatten.

4. Broil for 6 minutes on each side and serve on top of buns with desired toppings.

5. Serve and enjoy!

Recipe 18: Chinese Chicken Noodle

Noodles are one and the same with Chinese cuisine. They are widely used and it may be so because they represent longevity. This is a great soup to have around in the wintry times as it is hearty.

Yield: 3

Cooking Time: 15 minutes

List of Ingredients:

- Fresh noodles (24 oz.)
- Garlic (6 cloves, minced)
- Oil (3 Tbsp.)
- Chicken Broth (4 ½ cups)
- Water (1 ½ cups)
- Mushrooms- shiitake (12, sliced)
- Carrots (12 slices)
- Baby bok choy (12)
- White Pepper (¼ tsp.)
- Salt (¼ tsp.)
- Chicken (12 oz., cooked and shredded)

Instructions:

Boil noodles till al dente, then rinse and drain. Put aside till needed. Stir fry garlic in oil till golden, put aside. Heat broth and water then add carrot, mushrooms, bok choy, salt and pepper to taste.

When veggies have cooked, remove from flame. Serve by putting noodles in bowl, followed by chicken then soup. Pour a dash of garlic oil on top to finish. You may also serve with red chili in soy sauce.

Recipe 19: Apricot Tequila Glazed Drumsticks

These glazed drumsticks are oh so yummy and are easy to whip up. The drumsticks are sweet and spicy and will become a favorite. These could replace traditional Buffalo wings and are crispy too.

Yield: 3

Cooking Time: 1 hour 10 minutes

List of Ingredients:

- Chicken drumsticks (6)
- Chile de arbol (2 Tbsp., crushed)
- Salt (¼ tsp.)
- Apricot preserves (1 ½ cups)
- Sauza Tequila Blanco (1/3 cup)
- Black pepper (¼ tsp.)

Instructions:

1. Set oven to 350°F.

2. Combine chile de arbol, tequila and preserves in a saucepan and cook for 10 minutes over a low flame.

3. Use pepper and salt to season chicken and put into a baking dish.

4. Use sauce to coat chicken and pour leftover into dish.

5. Bake for 60 minutes until crisp and thoroughly cooked.

Recipe 20: Moo Shu Chicken Wraps

This Asian inspired wrap uses chicken moo shu instead of pork. The mixture is quick to put together and is rich in fiber.

Yield: 4

Cooking Time: 25 minutes

List of Ingredients:

- Chicken breasts (12 oz., halved)
- Olive oil (2 tsp.)
- Onion (1, chopped)
- Black pepper (¼ tsp.)
- Tortillas (4, whole grain)
- Broccoli florets (2 cups)
- Ginger (½ tsp., ground)
- Hoisin sauce (3 Tbsp.)

AAAAAAAAAAAAAAAAAAAAAAAAAAAAAAAAAAAAAA

Instructions:

1. Set oven to 350°F. Slice chicken into strips and put aside till needed. Put tortillas into foil, wrap and bake for 10 minutes until tortillas softened.

2. Heat half of oil in a skillet and add onion, pepper, broccoli and ginger to pot. Cook for 5 minutes then take vegetables from skillet and put aside.

3. Add leftover oil to skillet and heat then add chicken and cook for 5 minutes. Return vegetables to skillet along with hoisin sauce. Stir to combine and cook until thoroughly heated.

4. Spoon chicken mix into tortillas and roll. Slice in half and serve.

Recipe 21: Chicken Tequila Fettuccine

This is one of those dishes you can pull out for a special occasion. The fettuccine is creamy and flavorful with an added ingredient that makes it extra special.

Yield: 4

Cooking Time: 30 minutes

List of Ingredients:

- Fettuccine pasta (16 oz.)
- Garlic (2 Tbsp., diced)
- Butter (3 Tbsp.)
- Tequila (3 Tbsp.)
- Soy sauce (3 Tbsp.)
- Red onion (¼ sliced)
- Yellow bell pepper (½, sliced)
- Whipping cream (1 ½ cups, heavy)
- Cilantro (1/3 cup, chopped)
- Jalapenos (2 Tbsp., diced)
- Chicken broth (½ cup)
- Lime juice (2 Tbsp.)
- Chicken breasts (1 ¼ lbs., boneless and skinless and cubed)
- Red bell pepper (1, sliced thin)
- Green bell pepper (½, sliced thin)

AAAAAAAAAAAAAAAAAAAAAAAAAAAAAAAAAAAAAAAAAA

Instructions:

1. Melt 2 Tbsp. butter in a saucepan and sauté garlic, jalapeno and cilantro then add tequila, lime juice and broth. Cook until mixture becomes pasty; put aside until needed.

2. Combine chicken with soy sauce and let sit for 5 minutes.

3. Heat skillet, melt butter and sauté bell peppers along with onion. Cook until vegetables are soft then put in chicken and cook until browned.

4. Combine with the rest of the vegetables in sauce pan and add cream and tequila. Cook until sauce thickens.

5. Prepare pasta as directed on package, drain and serve topped with chicken mixture.

Recipe 22: Chicken Taco Salad

This tasty taco salad is great for lunch or dinner. You could add more things to your salad if you please. The mixture could even be had with freshly baked Paleo tortillas.

Yield: 3-4

Cooking Time: 30 minutes

List of Ingredients:

- Chicken breasts (1 lb., sliced)

Spice Blend:

- Water (1 cup, water)
- Paprika (1 tsp.)
- Onion Powder (1 Tbsp.)
- Chili powder (1 Tbsp.)
- Salt (½ tsp.)
- Dried oregano (2 tsp.)
- Ground cumin (1 Tbsp.)

Dressing:

- Tomato sauce (3/4 cup)
- Avocado (1)
- Lime (½ juiced)

Salad:

- Black olives (1 can, cut)
- Salad greens (1 bunch)
- Bell pepper- red (1, seeds removed and diced)
- Salsa (1 cup)

AA

Instructions:

Use a large skillet to cook chicken until browned. Combine all seasonings in a bowl and add water; whisk mixture together. Pour mixture onto chicken and cook for about 15 minutes until liquid has reduced.

Blend tomato juice, avocado and lime juice until smooth. Place salad greens in a container and top with black olives, red pepper, salsa, chicken and dressing. Serve and enjoy!

Recipe 23: Plantain Chip Nachos

These are quick and tasty when you are in the mood for some nachos. The plantain chips pair excellently with these toppings. You can add more toppings if you like.

Yield: 4

Cooking Time: 10 minutes

List of Ingredients:

- Plantain Chips (12 oz.)
- Chicken (1 cup, cooked)
- Goat Cheese (1 1/3 cups)
- Avocadoes (2, diced)
- Salsa (8 Tbsp.)
- Black Olives (8 Tbsp.)

AAAAAAAAAAAAAAAAAAAAAAAAAAAAAAAAAAAAAAAAAAA

Instructions:

Set oven to 325°F and put chips on a lined greased baking sheet. Put meat and cheese on top and bake for 5 minutes until chips are golden and cheese has melted.

Remove from the heat and top with avocado, salsa and olives. Serve and enjoy!

Recipe 24: Chicken and Avocado Tostadas

These are similar to tacos and they are absolutely delicious. These shells are so easy to make, you will be making them over and over again.

Yield: 4-6

Cooking Time: 30 minutes

List of Ingredients:

- Avocadoes (3, peeled and mashed)
- Cilantro (¼ cup, chopped)
- Black pepper (¼ tsp.)
- Roasted Chicken (2 cups, chopped)
- Lime juice (½ tsp.)
- Salt (¼ tsp.)
- Pico de gallo (1 cup)
- Smoked Paprika (¼ tsp.)

Tostada Shells:

- Almond flour (2 cups)
- Cayenne pepper (¼ tsp.)
- Olive oil (2 ¼ Tbsp.)
- Salt (½ tsp.)
- Eggs (2)

Instructions:

Mix lime juice, avocadoes and cilantro together in a bowl. Put together paprika, chicken and lime juice in a separate bowl.

Make tostados by mixing cayenne, flour and salt together then put in oil and eggs and form dough. Divide into 6 equal parts, roll flat and heat 2 Tbsp. of oil in a skillet and cook tostados for 1 minute on both sides.

Put on hand towels to remove excess oil. Lay tostados flat and add avocado mix then put in chicken and top with salsa.

Recipe 25: Chicken and Cornmeal Dumplings

This one pot meal is full of protein and is bursting with flavor. These homemade dumplings are filling and pair deliciously with the chicken. Get that slow cooker out and try this wonderful meal.

Yield: 2

Cooking Time: 4-6 hours

List of Ingredients:

- Carrots (2, sliced thin)
- Corn kernels (1/3 cup)
- Garlic (2 cloves, diced)
- Black pepper (¼ tsp.)
- Chicken broth (1 cup, low salt)
- Flour (1 Tbsp.)
- Celery (1 stalk, sliced thin)
- Onion (½, sliced thin)
- Rosemary (1 tsp.)
- Chicken thighs (2, skin removed)
- Milk (½ cup, fat free)

For dumplings:

- Flour (¼ cup)
- Baking powder (½ tsp.)
- Egg white (1)
- Canola oil (1 Tbsp.)
- Cornmeal (¼ cup)
- Salt (¼ tsp.)
- Milk (1 Tbsp., fat free)

AAAAAAAAAAAAAAAAAAAAAAAAAAAAAAAAAAAAAAAA

Instructions:

1. Prepare dumplings by combining flour, baking powder, salt and cornmeal in a bowl. Combine milk, oil and egg white in a separate bowl. Add wet mixture to dry mix and stir to combine until moist.

2. Add carrots, corn, garlic, black pepper, celery, onion and rosemary to slow cooker. Then put in chicken and broth.

3. Set on low and cook for 7-8 hours or on high for 3-4 hours.

4. Remove chicken from slow cooker and cool for 5 minutes then remove bones and chop chicken and return to cooker.

5. Combine flour and milk and add to slow cooker. Use spoon to drop dumplings into cooker. Cook for an additional 20-25 minutes.

6. Serve hot and enjoy!

Recipe 26: Mexican Chicken Soup with Cheddar Cheese Chips

This soup is definitely even better with the cheese chips. Choose your favorite kind of cheese and try different flavors if you please.

Yield: 4-6

Cooking Time: 3 hours 5 minutes

List of Ingredients:

- Chicken broth (6 cups)
- Yellow Onion (½, chopped)
- Garlic (4 cloves, sliced)
- Tomato juice (1 cup)
- Coriander (1 tsp.)
- Whole chicken (1, skinned)
- Cilantro (½ cup)
- Carrots (3, sliced)
- Poblano pepper (1, seeds removed, diced)
- Tomatoes (3, chopped)
- Lime juice- freshly squeezed (¼ tsp.)
- Sea salt (2 Tbsp.)

For topping:

- Black beans (½ Cup)
- Sour cream (¼ Cup)
- Cheddar cheese chips (½ Cup)
- Avocado (¼ Cup)

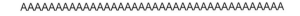

Instructions:

Put all ingredients for soup into a crock pot excluding cilantro and lime juice. Set on high and cook for 3 hours. Take chicken from pot and shred. Throw away bones and put shredded chicken in pot.

Add cilantro and lime juice. Cook for an additional hour. Serve with cheese chips and toppings except avocado. Avocado is to be served on the side.

About the Author

Molly Mills always knew she wanted to feed people delicious food for a living. Being the oldest child with three younger brothers, Molly learned to prepare meals at an early age to help out her busy parents. She just seemed to know what spice went with which meat and how to make sauces that would dress up the blandest of pastas. Her creativity in the kitchen was a blessing to a family where money was tight and making new meals every day was a challenge.

Molly was also a gifted athlete as well as chef and secured a Lacrosse scholarship to Syracuse University. This was a blessing to her family as she was the first to go to college and at little cost to her parents. She took full advantage of her college education and earned a business degree. When she graduated, she joined her culinary skills and business acumen into a successful catering business. She wrote her first e-book after a customer asked if she could pay for several of her recipes. This sparked the entrepreneurial spirit in Mills and she thought if one person wanted them, then why not share the recipes with the world!

Molly lives near her family's home with her husband and three children and still cooks for her family every chance she gets. She plays Lacrosse with a local team made up of her old teammates from college and there are always some tasty nibbles on the ready after each game.

Don't Miss Out!

Scan the QR-Code below and you can sign up to receive emails whenever Molly Mills publishes a new book. There's no charge and no obligation.

Sign Me Up

https://molly.gr8.com

Printed in Great Britain
by Amazon